Learn about Telling the Time with

Hickory
Dickory
Dock

Author's Note:

This book and others in the same series
grew out of a desire to make learning fun.
At the back you will find some games and activities
that will help children learn more about telling the time.
Feel free to adapt them to your own needs.
I have also included the original version of
the Hickory Dickory Dock nursery rhyme.

First published in 2001 by
Franklin Watts
96 Leonard Street
London EC2A 4XD

Franklin Watts Australia
56 O'Riordan Street
Alexandria
NSW 2015

ISBN 0 7496 4302 1 (hardback)
ISBN 0 7496 4378 1 (paperback)

Text copyright © Saviour Pirotta 2001
Illustrations copyright © Mike Gordon 2001
Colour by Carl Gordon

A CIP catalogue record for this book is available from the British Library.

Printed in Hong Kong, China

Learn about Telling the Time with
Hickory Dickory Dock

by Saviour Pirotta
illustrated by Mike Gordon

W
FRANKLIN WATTS
LONDON•SYDNEY

Hickory dickory dock,
The mice looked at the clock.

The clock struck one!

The clock struck two!

The clock struck three!

The clock struck four!

The clock struck five!

The clock struck six!

The clock struck seven!

The clock struck eight!

The clock struck nine!

The clock struck ten!

The clock struck eleven!

The clock struck twelve!

Hickory dickory dock.

Hickory Dickory Dock

Hickory dickory dock,

The mouse ran up the clock.

The clock struck one,

The mouse ran down,

Hickory dickory dock.

Games you can play

Some fun activities to help children learn more about telling the time.

THE MIMING TIMES

Learning to tell the time involves two distinct skills: recognising the numbers on the face of the clock, and understanding that each number represents a different time of day. Here's a musical game that will help children get to grips with both.

1. Find a musical instrument that you can bang on, like a drum or a tambourine. Every time you bang on it, the children must count how many times you hit it.

2. When you've hit it several times, declare the time and announce a suitable activity. For example, hit the drum four times and call out, 'Four o'clock. Time for tea.'

3. The children then mime drinking tea until they hear the next lot of drumbeats.

4. Vary the ideas, and don't be afraid to suggest fun activities such as 'Time to pick daisies' or 'Time to give Granny a kiss'.

5. Always end with 'Time for bed' so the players will recognise that the game is over.

MY FAVOURITE TIME OF DAY

1. Get children to draw large clocks on sheets of paper, using paints, crayons or felt-tips. Help them write in the numbers.

2. Discuss with them their favourite time of day and what they like doing at that time. Then help them draw the hands pointing to their favourite time.

3. Afterwards, they can decorate the face of the clock with drawings showing their favourite activities.

IT'S THAT TIME OF DAY

This time-based activity is for a special day.

1. Using a clock that chimes the hour, record all the times of the day on a cassette tape. Do not record them in sequence.

2. With face paints, draw clocks on the children's faces, making sure that all hours of the day are represented. You can have more than one child with the same time of day drawn on their face.

3. At various intervals, play the cassette so that it announces an hour. Children with the corresponding clock drawn on their face can then collect a special treat. This might be a sweet, or a piggyback ride, or whatever they would most enjoy.

TIME FOR TELLING

Books can be used as a way of exploring the theme of time.

1. Help children to collect all the books in your library connected with time. Include non-fiction titles, modern stories, classics, picture books and poems.

2. Discuss with them how they can tell the books are about time. What can they see on the cover or in the illustrations inside? Make a display and discuss the books.

3. Tell a story about time. There are many traditional tales about the subject, often featuring funny characters trying to do too much in too little time. Poems are useful too, and can round off the day nicely when it's time to go home or go to bed.